Dedication

The "American Standard 100+ Bartender's Handbook" is dedicated to all who choose to use it. My thanks to numerous bartenders all over the country who were questioned about the most-asked-for cocktails and whose opinions are greatly appreciated.

My particular thanks to Mr. Richard W. Kruckman and Rosendo L. (Joe) Marquez.

The cocktails depicted in the American Standard 100+ Bartender's Handbook are actual drinks made by Master Mixologist Richard W. Kruckman. They were served in Libby glasses and the photographs were taken in the cocktail lounge of the Brigadoon Restaurant in Vacaville, California. I greatly appreciate all the courtesies extended to me by Mr. Steve Seghetti, owner of the Brigadoon.

Since I am part American Indian, a portion of the profits from this book will be donated to Indian causes of my choice.

Tommy Murphy

—photography by Bob Hoenig and Frank Kopecky

Introduction

Someone said "necessity is the mother of invention." Compare our bar guide to any you have ever seen and you will see the need for the "American Standard 100+ Bartender's Handbook."

Except for a few exotic drinks, all the recipes herein are selections from an extensive survey and the experience of Mr. Murphy.

The 100+ recipes contained in this book are the most-asked-for cocktails.

Our endeavor is to make your cocktails easy and fun to make and to lead you to an adventure in delicious refreshment. We feel the information compiled in our handbook will assist you to a more knowledgeable and sophisticated lifestyle.

This reference book
— has both a full-color illustration and a detailed recipe;
— is water resistant to guarantee longer book life;
— has large print for easier readability;
— is short and to the point for simplicity;
— has no far-out recipes that won't ever be used.

American Standard 100+ Bartender's Handbook

The Complete Bar Guide

102 cocktail recipes with

full-color illustrations

of how they should look

by

Tommy Murphy

**Created and owned
by
T.A.M. Creative Publications
Vacaville, California 95688
U.S.A.**

American Standard 100+ Bartender's Handbook
by
Tommy Murphy

©MCMLXXXII

Thomas A. Murphy

Second Printing, June 1983

Published and Printed by
Hanseatic Press, San Francisco

Copyright in:	U.S.A.
	Great Britain
Applied for in:	Australia
	New Zealand
	Canada

Table of Contents

Alphabetical Index by Drink Name

Alphabetical Index by Drink Name (cont.)

Alphabetical Index by Drink Name (cont.)

Alphabetical Index by Drink Name (cont.)

Cocktails by Liquor Content

10

Cocktails by Liquor Content (cont.)

Cocktails by Liquor Content (cont.)

Cocktails by Liquor Content (cont.)

Liquor Definitions

Alcohol: ethyl alcohol base for all liquor made from grains, grapes, fruit, cane, and potatoes (grain neutral spirits).

Brandy: distilled from grapes and fermented fruit mash.

Cognac: fine filtered and aged brandy; originated in Cognac region of France. NOTE: All cognac is brandy but all brandy is not cognac.

Gin: grain neutral spirits with juniper berry juice added. Some gins contain more herbs for taste and aroma (Bombay). Two types of gin are London and Holland. Holland gin is heavier and made by a different process. Gin originated in Holland as a medicine, a mild diuretic. Americans are more familiar with London dry gin.

Rum: distilled from sugar cane. Originated in the Canary Islands. Rum drinks are considered very good for colds: contain vitamins C and D. This is the primary reason for both the English and American navies having a rum ration in years past to ward off scurvy.

Tequila: made in Mexico; distilled from fermented mescal cactus.

Vodka: grain neutral spirits, base of all liquors. Example: it is whiskey after four years aging; gin after juniper berries are added.

Whiskey: grain neutral spirits with four or more years aging in charred barrels.

Bourbon: originated in Kentucky; 51% or more corn mash aged in new charred barrels. Name derived from Bourbon County, Kentucky.

Rye Whiskey: distilled from mash; 51% rye or more.

Bottled in Bond Whiskey: government guaranteed 100-proof—50% alcohol.

Blended Whiskey: straight whiskies and grain neutral spirits, not less than 80-proof.

Canadian Whisky: from rye, corn, and barley, made only in Canada, blended under government supervision to be light in body, mild in flavor.

Scotch Whisky: product of Scotland; number one in their economy. All scotch is made from barley malt and grain neutral spirits; flavor derived from being contaminated with smoke from barley malt sprouts being dried.

Irish Whiskey: Irish product. Made like scotch except for the open driers for barley sprouts (not coming in contact with smoke).

Bar Tips

10 to 15 shakes of mixing cup equivalent to 10 to 15 seconds on blender.

Simple Syrup may be substituted with Sugar or White Karo Syrup.

Taste juices and mixes to be sure they are fresh.

On an assorted order, make all flat drinks first, then fruit drinks, then cream drinks; pour beer last.

To peel lemon, cut off both ends into the meat of the fruit. Lightly force spoon handle under peel, work handle around under peel until completely free from fruit. Cut peel to desired size for twist and garnish.

Many tomato and fruit juice-based drinks should have the ice added last to minimize ice melt time.

Never try to make more than five drinks at one time in an average size blender.

Rinse blender, mixing cup, and strainer between different drinks.

Always use ice scoop; never your hands.

Swizzle sticks may be used as an effective cooling tool by holding between both palms and rotating.

Ditch is whiskey and water; *Branch Water* also means whiskey and water.

Water-back means water-chaser.

Always fill glass with ice unless recipe specifies amount.

Virgin Mary is spiced tomato juice with no liquor.

Up means in a stemmed glass.

Over means poured over ice.

Neat means straight, no ice or anything else.

Rocks mean ice.

Dry means little or no sugar. Sweet is the opposite of dry. *Brut* is extra-dry.

Perfect — drink contains both dry and red vermouth.

An easy way to flame a cocktail: use ½ tsp. of sugar saturated with Irish Whiskey, Chartreuse, or appropriate alcohol; heat and flame; transfer flame to top of drink.

Common Measurements

Dash	⅛ oz.
½ Pint	8 oz.
Pint	16 oz.
Fifth	25.6 oz.
Quart	32 oz.
Half Gallon	64 oz.
Magnum	52 oz.
Pony Keg	4½ gallons
Quarter Keg	8 gallons
Half Barrel	16 gallons
Barrel	32 gallons
Bar Ice Scoop	6 oz.

30 milliliters	=	1 fluid oz.
.24 liters	=	1 cup
.47 liters	=	1 pint
.95 liters	=	1 quart
3.8 liters	=	1 USA Gallon
4.5 liters	=	1 Imperial Gallon
114 liters	=	30 USA Gallons (Barrel)
750 milliliters	=	1/5 USA Gallon (25 oz.)

Useful Bar Tools

Mixing Cup, metal preferably
  24 to 32 oz.

Shaker cup, metal and glass pair —
  used when blender unavailable

Strainer, woven wire or spring

Bar spoon — long handle

Blender

Shot glass

Pour spouts; good ones that don't leak

Ice scoop — approximately 6 oz. size

Muddling stick

Ice mallet — small

Ice pick

Paring knife

Garnish spears or toothpicks

Cocktail Mixes

Sweetened Lemon Juice
Orange Juice
Grapefruit Juice
Tomato Juice
Cream
Coca-Cola
Ginger Ale
7-Up
Simple Syrup
Soda
Tonic
Triple Sec
Orange Bitters
Orange Flower Water
  (Ramos Fizz)
Rose's Lime Juice
Orgeat (substitute with
  Creme de Almond or Orzata)

Garnishes

Cherries
Olives
Lemons
Limes
Pearl Onions
Orange Slices
Mint
Cinnamon Sticks
Celery Sticks and
  Hearts
Nutmeg

Liqueurs Most Commonly Used

Green and White Creme de Menthe
  (peppermint flavor)

White and Dark Creme de Cacao
  (light chocolate flavor)

Kahlua *(coffee flavor)*

Sloe Gin *(cherry flavor)*

Amaretto *(chocolate and coffee flavor —light, nutty)*

Cherry and Blackberry flavored Brandies

Blue Curacao *(spearmint flavor)*

Orange Curacao *(orange flavor)*

Drambuie *(honey-sweet scotch flavor)*

Creme de Almond *(light cherry and nut flavor)*

Creme de Banana *(banana flavor)*

Galliano *(light, honey licorice flavor)*

Wines Used in Bars

White Vermouth
  (very dry—aperitif)

Red Vermouth
  (slightly sweet)

Dinner Red and White Wines
  *(to serve or mix with soda water and fruit
  juices as a cooler)*

Champagne, Sparkling Burgundy

Dessert wines: Port, Marsala, Muscatel
  Some sacramental wines make fine
  dessert wines.

Dessert Wines

Wines such as Port, Muscatel, and Marsala
are made from naturally sweet varieties of
grapes. In California, it is against the law to
add sugar.

Sparkling Wines

Champagne, Sekt, Spumante, Espumante,
Shampanskoe, Mousseux, non-Red and
labeled Brut, Sec (dry and extra-dry, Demi-Sec
or Doux) (less than 1.5% sugar).

Flavored Wines
(Anthocyanin Pigments)

Cinchona — bitter taste
Retsina — turpentine taste

White or Dry Vermouth, Red Vermouth (sweet), Byrrh, Dubonnet, Thunderbird, and Silver Satin all contain added flavors, herbs, etc.

Red Table Wines

Grape varieties are: Barbera, Cabernet, Ruby Cabernet, Concord, Gamay, Pinot Noir, Zinfandel, Grignolino, Petite Sarah, Pinot St. George, Charbono, Grenache, and Nebbiolo.

Red and white table wines are almost void of sugar (dry) and a point to remember is the dryer the wine the lower the alcohol content, unlike some dessert wines which are sweet and the alcohol content high.

Sacramental Wines

Usually sweet and most do not exceed 18% alcohol per standards established by the Catholic church in Spain and Italy and followed by the U.S.A.

White Table Wines
(Mostly from California)

Pinot-Chardonnay, Chenin Blanc (White Pinot), Emerald Riesling, Folle Blanche, French Colombard, Gewürztraminer, Grey Riesling, Malvasia Bianca, Pinot Blanc, Sauvignon Blanc, Semillon, Sylvaner, White Riesling, Johannisberg Riesling.

The grape varieties in making some white wines are: Aligote, Burger, Clairette Blanche, Green Hungarian, Palomino, Saint Emilion, and Thompson Seedless.

Rosé Wines

Made from grapes that do not release the darker red juices, such as Aramon, Grenache, Grignolino, and Napa Gamay.

Author's Comment:
   I suggest that you continue to experiment to find a wine that suits you. It isn't at all necessary to destroy your budget to find a very nice wine. It is presently accepted to drink the wine of your choice, whether white or red with fish, red meat, or fowl.
   Let your palate be your guide.

Easy To Make Recipes which will cut your home entertainment cost.

Amaretto Liqueur

3 Cups Sugar
2 Cups Water
½ Cup Bourbon
3 Cups Vodka
3 Tblsp. Coconut Extract
Peel from 1 lemon
6 Teaspoons Almond Extract
1 Tblsp. Chocolate Extract
1 Tblsp. Vanilla Extract
Boil lemon peel and sugar 20 mins. Add flavors and liqueurs; mix well; allow to cool before bottling.

Kahlua Liqueur

16 Teaspoons Instant Coffee in 1 Qt. Water
Stir in 3 Cups Sugar, Boil 20 mins.
Add 11 ozs. Vodka
Add 3 Teaspoons Cacao or Coconut Syrup
Stir well. Allow to cool before bottling.

Alexander

Cocktail Glass   5½ oz.
Mixing Cup, 4 oz. Ice
½ oz. White Creme de Cacao
½ oz. Gin
2 oz. Cream
Blend and strain

NOTE:
The above recipe is the basic true recipe. Alexanders can be changed to "call" or desire by changing the liquor.

Angel's Tip

Cordial Glass   1 oz.
½ filled with Brown Creme
de Cacao
½ filled with Cream
Place cream on top poured over
spoon.
Spear cherry and place on top.

NOTE:
*Angel's Tip is a King Alphonse
with the speared cherry placed
on top of the glass.*

Angel's Tit

Cordial Glass   1 oz.

¾ oz. Maraschino Liqueur

¼ oz. Fresh Cream (whipped, if possible)

Pour liqueur into glass.

Place cream on top of liqueur by pouring on back of spoon, to keep cream on top.

Place cherry in exact center.

NOTE:

A large or heavy cherry may have to be speared and placed across the glass to prevent it from sinking into the drink.

B & B

Cordial Glass   1 oz.
½ filled with Benedictine
½ filled with Brandy
Float brandy on top of
benedictine.
To float brandy, pour over back
of spoon.

NOTE:
B & B can be purchased as a
liqueur already mixed, but it is
preferable to mix your own from
the separate ingredients.

Bacardi

Cocktail Glass   5½ oz.
Mixing Cup, 4 oz. Ice
1½ oz. Sweet Lemon Juice
½ oz. Grenadine
1 oz. Light Rum
Blend 15 to 30 seconds and pour.

NOTE:
The Bacardi is exactly like a
Daiquiri except for the Grenadine
added for color.

Banshee

Cocktail Glass   5½ oz.
Mixing Cup, 4 oz. Ice
2 oz. Cream
½ oz. White Creme de Cacao
½ oz. Creme de Banana
Blend and strain

NOTE:
Fresh banana and a full ounce of White Creme de Cacao may be substituted.

Between the Sheets

Cocktail Glass   5½ oz.

Mixing Cup, 4 oz. Ice

¾ oz. Light Rum

¾ oz. Brandy

¾ oz. Triple Sec

½ oz. Lemon Juice

Blend with ice and strain.

Rim glass with sugar.

NOTE:

Very few drinks call for sugar on the rim of glass; the Side Car is another. It adds a certain delight to the drink. Excellent after-dinner drink.

Black Russian

Rock or Manhattan Glass   5 oz.
½ oz. Vodka
½ oz. Kahlua

NOTE:
This drink may be separated by pouring the vodka over the back of a spoon; vodka, being lighter, will float on top.

Bloody Maria

Highball Glass half-filled with
Ice   12 oz.
1 oz. Tequila
2 oz. Tomato Juice
1 tsp. Lemon Juice
⅛ oz. Tabasco Sauce
Dash Celery Salt
Mix tequila, tomato juice, and
lemon in serving glass. Add
celery salt. Garnish with lemon
slice. Guest may add tabasco
sauce.

NOTE:
*The difference between a Bloody
Maria and a Bloody Mary is the
use of tequila instead of vodka.
Also, you may mix all
ingredients first, leaving room
for ice to be added.*

Bloody Mary

Highball Glass — Ice   12 oz.
1 oz. Vodka
Fill with Tomato Juice
Garnish with lime squeeze
Drop fruit in drink

For spice — add Worcestershire
Sauce, salt, pepper, celery salt,
and tabasco.
Also may be garnished with
celery heart.

Blue Angel

Cocktail Glass or Tulip Glass

5½ oz.

Mixing Cup, 4 oz. Ice

½ oz. Blue Curacao

½ oz. Brandy

½ oz. White Creme de Cacao

½ oz. Lemon Juice

½ oz. Cream

Blend and strain

NOTE:

This drink is very tasty and beautifully different.

Blue Devil

Cocktail Glass or Tulip Glass
5½ oz.
1½ oz. Gin
½ oz. Blue Curacao
½ oz. Lemon Juice
Blend gin, curacao with ice.
Strain.
Garnish with lemon slice.

NOTE:
Another beautiful drink to try.
Deceivingly tasty.

Blue Hawaiian

Tulip Glass   5½ oz.

Mixing Cup, 5 oz. Ice

2 oz. Sweet Lemon Juice

1 oz. Pineapple Juice

1 oz. Light Rum

½ oz. Blue Curacao

Blend 15 to 20 seconds.

Garnish with strip of pineapple.

NOTE:

Probably the most popular of all blue cocktails.

Brandy Alexander

Cocktail Glass   5½ oz.

Mixing Cup, 4 oz. Ice

½ oz. Brown Creme de Cacao

½ oz. Brandy

2 oz. Cream

Blend and strain

Sprinkle lightly with nutmeg.

NOTE:

The difference from the original Alexander: brandy instead of gin.

Brave Bull

Manhattan Glass   5 oz.
Glass ¾ full of Ice
½ oz. Tequila
½ oz. Kahlua

NOTE:
Sometimes a dash of soda will be asked for; if so, make it a very small dash.

Bull Shot

Highball Glass   8 oz.
4 oz. chilled Beef Consomme
1½ oz. Vodka
Pour over rocks.
Garnish with lemon slice.

NOTE:
*A very good drink to be made
and served at home.*
Excellent cold weather drink.

Cape Codder

Highball Glass, filled ¾ with
Ice   8 oz.
1 oz. Vodka
Fill balance of glass with
Cranberry Juice.

NOTE:
The Cape Codder was originated
in the New England states — a
spin-off of the Cranberry Bogs.
I find it a very tasty, attractive
cocktail, and so easy to make.

    In later years, cranapple juice
has been substituted for the pure
cranberry juice.

Capuccino

Tumbler   (8 oz. Glass)
1 oz. Medium Sweet Chocolate
1 tsp. Instant Coffee
1 tsp. Sugar
6½ oz. Hot Milk
Float 1 oz. Brandy

NOTE:
Capuccino is very controversial.
The recipe can vary slightly with
each bartender. The above recipe
is as close to the original as could
be found.

Champagne Cocktail

Champagne Glass (Cocktail)

3½ oz.

½ oz. Simple Syrup

1 dash Bitters

Fill with chilled champagne.

Garnish with lemon twist.

Drop lemon peel into drink.

NOTE:
A very good cocktail for two or more people, because most cocktail lounges will charge for the complete bottle of champagne. If only one person is ordering, it is a good idea to ask if you must purchase the whole bottle of champagne.

Champagne Punch

The most important thing to remember about preparing a punch is knowing your guests. There are many people who would prefer a non-alcoholic refreshment. If this be the case, replace champagne with carbonated soft drinks, soda water, ginger ale, strawberry-flavored soda, Fresca, etc. You may continue to use pineapple, apple, or orange juice as a base. A good punch can be made by using one's own ingenuity and good common sense (use your imagination). It is good etiquette to have both punches and mark one bowl non-alcoholic.

My Favorite:

Champagne Punch

All ingredients chilled
4 bottles Pink Champagne
(inexpensive)
4 qts. Club Soda
2 qts. 7-Up
2 qts. Orange Juice
½ lbs Sugar (Granulated)
Pre-freeze 4 ice-cube trays of
Cherry Juice or Cranberry
Juice. Float on top in punch
bowl. Serves 30.

NOTE:

Champagne will marry perfectly with any fruit juice and/or carbonated beverage. You may need to multiply and mix separately for amount necessary for more guests. If spiking is desired, use vodka to taste. Garnish with cucumber peel if desired.

Chi-Chi

Collins Glass ½ filled with Ice
11 oz.
2 oz. Creme of Coconut Syrup
3 oz. Pineapple Juice
1 oz. Vodka
Blend approximately 15 seconds
and pour.
Garnish with strip of pineapple.

NOTE:
Same as a Pina Colada except you use vodka instead of light rum.

Coffee Royal

Coffee Mug or Cup   8 oz.
1 tsp. Sugar
1 oz. Brandy
Pour into cup
Fill up with hot coffee.
Twist of lemon dropped into cup.

NOTE:
A good tip is to allow the cup or mug to preheat by running hot water over it. The drink will be much more enjoyable for a longer period of time.

Cuba Libre

14 oz. Collins Glass ½ filled with
Ice
2 oz. Golden Rum
½ Lime squeezed and dropped
into drink.
Fill with Cola.

NOTE:
1 teaspoon of 151 proof rum can
be placed on top if desired.

Daiquiri

Cocktail Glass   6 oz.
Mixing Cup, 4 oz. Ice
½ oz. Sweet Lemon Juice
1 oz. Light Rum
Blend 15 to 20 seconds.
Pour

NOTE:
The grenadine is missing;
otherwise, it would be a Bacardi.
The Frozen Daiquiri can be
found under 'F' in this book.

Devil's Delight
(Mr. Murphy's original)

Cocktail Glass   5½ oz.
Mixing Cup, 4 oz. Ice
1½ oz. Orange Juice
1 oz. Amaretto or Kahlua
½ oz. Cream
Blend 15 to 20 seconds.
Strain

NOTE:
This is not a weight watcher's
cocktail.

Dirty Mother

Rock Glass (Manhattan) ½ full of
Ice
1 oz. Brandy
1 oz. Kahlua
1 oz. Cream
Stir and serve

NOTE:
This drink is a spin-off of the
White Russian, replacing vodka
with brandy.

Dry Manhattan

Stemmed Manhattan or Rock
Glass 5½ oz.
Fill Glass ¾ with Ice
1½ oz. Whiskey
¼ oz. Dry Vermouth
Garnish with olive.

NOTE:
Dry Scotch Manhattan is the
same as Dry Manhattan except
scotch is used instead of bourbon.

Dubonnet Cocktail

Cocktail Glass   3½ oz.
1¼ oz. Dubonnet Wine
1¼ oz. Gin
Stir well in ice and strain into glass.
Garnish with lemon peel.

NOTE:
An appropriate aperitif or before dinner cocktail.

Flaming
Irish Coffee

Mug, Cup or Tumbler   8 oz.

Hot Coffee

Gently place ¾ oz. Irish Whiskey
on top of coffee.

In teaspoon, mix ½ tsp. Sugar
saturated with Irish Whiskey.
Hold small flame under spoon
until contents ignite.

Hold ignited spoon to top of
coffee to create flame in cup.

NOTE:
When you become more profi-
cient at preparing this drink,
you can be the bartender with a
flare.

French Kiss

Stemmed Glass   4½ oz.
2 oz. Sweet Vermouth
2 oz. Dry Vermouth
Pour over rocks in glass.
Rim glass with lemon peel.
Drop peel into drink.

The drink pictured was blended.
Do not strain if blended.

NOTE:
Only very good vermouth should be used to make this wine cocktail.

French 75

Collins Glass   11 oz.
Mixing Cup, 5 oz. Ice
2 oz. Sweet Lemon Juice
1 oz. Gin
Blend
Finish filling glass with
Champagne.

NOTE:
Like the Champagne Cocktail, in
some bars you may be charged
for a complete bottle of
champagne.

Frozen Daiquiri

6 oz. Cocktail or Champagne Glass

Mixing Cup, 5 oz. Ice

2 oz. Sweet Lemon Juice

1 oz. Light Rum

½ oz. Triple Sec

Blend approximately 2 minutes.
Spoon snow into glass; heap up snow.
Shape by placing same size glass over heaping snow.
Garnish with cherry; stand 2 straws in glass.

NOTE:
The extra amount of ice, plus longer blending time, makes the cocktail thick enough to spoon.

Fruit Daiquiri

Tulip Glass   6 oz.
Mixing Cup, 4 oz. Ice
1½ to 2 oz. Light Rum
½ to 1 tsp. Sugar
3 oz. Strawberries, Melon,
Banana, or any other fruit.
Blend 15 to 20 seconds.
Pour and serve with bar straw.

NOTE:
Add 1 teaspoon of 151 proof rum
on top if desired.

Gimlet

Stemmed Rock or Manhattan
Glass 4½ oz.
Mixing Cup, 4 oz. Ice
1½ oz. Gin
½ oz. Rose's Lime Juice
Stir in cup to chill
Strain and pour
Garnish with lime slice

NOTE:
This drink is in the top ten in
popularity throughout the U.S.A.

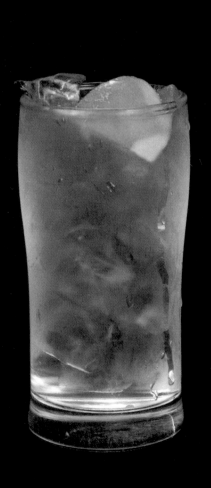

Gin and Tonic

Highball Glass filled with Ice
8 oz.
1 oz. Gin
Fill with Tonic
Lime Squeeze garnish

NOTE:
Any liquor may be used in tonic.
English origination in India to
ward off malaria, using only
Bombay Gin. A very nice cocktail,
made with any gin.
One of top ten in popularity in
the U.S.A.

Gin Buck

Highball Glass ½ filled with Ice
8 oz.
1½ oz. Gin
½ oz. Sweet Lemon Juice
Finish filling glass with Ginger
Ale
Stir and serve
Garnish with lemon slice.

NOTE:
This old-time cocktail originated about the time of the Side Car, at the turn of the century.

Gin Presbyterian

Highball Glass filled with Ice
8 oz.
1 oz. Gin
½ filled with Ginger Ale
Complete fill with Soda.

NOTE:
Any liquor can be called for in a Presbyterian.
The above recipe is the original Presbyterian.

Godfather

Rock or Manhattan Glass
5 oz.
almost filled with Ice
1½ oz. Scotch
½ oz. Amaretto

NOTE:
A spin-off of Drambuie; very
sweet, but tasty.

Gold Cadillac

Cocktail Glass   4½ oz.
Mixing Cup, 4 oz. Ice
2 oz. Cream
½ oz. White Creme de Cacao
½ oz. Galliano
Blend and strain

NOTE:
A slight flavor of licorice.
Not for weight watchers.

Grasshopper

Cocktail Glass   4½ oz.
Mixing Cup, 4 oz. Ice
2 oz. Cream
½ oz. White Creme de Cacao
½ oz. Green Creme de Menthe
Blend and strain

NOTE:
Colorful ladies' drink, although
men enjoy it also.

Greyhound

Highball Glass filled with Ice
8 oz.
1 oz. Vodka
Fill with Grapefruit Juice.

NOTE:
This drink is sometimes ordered
in a bar as "Vodkagrape."

Harvey Wallbanger

Highball Glass filled with Ice
8 oz.
1 oz. Vodka
Fill with Orange Juice.
Top with Galliano.

NOTE:
A licorice-flavored Screwdriver.

Highball

Highball Glass, full of Ice   8 oz.
1 oz. Whiskey
Fill with Ginger Ale.

NOTE:
The original Highball was
mixed with ginger ale.
In some parts of the country, the
term highball has mistakenly
replaced the word cocktail.

Hot Buttered Rum

Mug or Cup   8 oz.
1 oz. Light or Dark Rum
1 tsp. Sugar
Fill with Hot Water
Add tab of Butter
Top with Cream
Sprinkle with Nutmeg

NOTE:
Preheat cup or mug for more lasting enjoyment.

Hot Toddy

8 oz. Tumbler
1 tsp. Sugar
2 oz. Brandy
Pour Hot Water and stir
1 slice Lemon
Cinnamon Stick

NOTE:
Preheat tumbler.

Irish Coffee

Mug or Cup   8 oz.
½ oz. Simple Syrup
1 oz. Irish Whisky
Fill with very hot Coffee.
Top with Whipped Cream.

NOTE:
Preheat mug or cup.
A little sprinkle of nutmeg may
be asked for.

John Collins

(Modern)

Collins Glass ¾ filled with Ice
11 oz.
2½ oz. Sweet Lemon Juice
1 oz. Whiskey (blended or
bourbon)
Fill up with Soda
Garnish with Lime or Lemon
slice.

NOTE:
See next page for the original
recipe.

John Collins

(Original)

Collins Glass ¾ full of Ice   11 oz.
2½ oz. Sweet Lemon Juice
1 oz. Dutch Jenever Gin
Fill to top with Soda.

NOTE:
Dutch Jenever Gin is the differ-
ence between John Collins
(Modern) and John Collins
(Original).

King Alphonse

Cordial Glass   1 oz.

Fill ½ with Brown Creme
de Cacao
Fill balance with Cream placed
gently on top of liqueur.
To keep separated, pour cream
over back of spoon.

NOTE:
No cherry — or King Alphonse
becomes an Angel's Tip.

Madras

Highball Glass with Ice   8 oz.
1 oz. Vodka
Fill glass with equal amounts of
Orange and Cranberry Juice.

NOTE:
The orange juice is the only
difference from the Cape Codder.

5$

659 02 Rum
90 02 lemon
60 Juice.
60
30

Mai Tai

Double Old-Fashioned or Double
Rock Glass   15 oz.
Mixing Cup ½ filled with Ice
1½ oz. Sweet Lemon Juice
½ oz. Orgeat or Almond Syrup
½ oz. Triple Sec
1 oz. Light Rum
Blend and pour. Garnish with
cherry or speared cherry and
lime slice.

NOTE:
*The above recipe is the one used
in most bars. Original is made
with 2 ozs. of rum and orzata
instead of orgeat or almond
syrup.*

Manhattan

Rock or Stemmed Manhattan
Glass 4½ oz.
Fill glass ¾ with Ice
1½ oz. Whiskey
¼ oz. Sweet Vermouth
Garnish with Cherry.

NOTE:
Scotch Manhattan same as
above except for the liquor.

Margarita

Cocktail or Margarita Glass

9 oz.

Mixing Cup, 5 oz. Ice

Moisten rim of glass with lime; salt rim

1½ oz. Sweet Lemon-Lime Juice

1 oz. Tequila

½ oz. Triple Sec

Blend 5 to 10 seconds and pour Garnish with squeeze of lime; drop into glass.

NOTE:
Very popular in the west but becoming more popular all over the U.S.A.

Martini— Extra Dry

Stemmed Manhattan or Cocktail Glass   3½ oz.

Mixing Cup, 5 oz. Ice

1½ oz. Gin

Dash of Dry Vermouth

Stir in cup a little longer to accumulate more water from melting ice since you are using less vermouth. Strain and garnish with cocktail olive.

NOTE:
U.S.A.'s most popular drink.

Martini — Up

Stemmed Manhattan or Cocktail
Glass   3½ oz.

Mixing Cup, 5 oz. Ice

1½ oz. Gin

¼ oz. Dry Vermouth

Stir while holding cup in hand to
help melt ice. Stir long enough to
assure water content to fill glass.
Strain into glass and serve.
Garnish with cocktail olive.

NOTE:
A Gibson is a Martini with onion
garnish instead of an olive.

Mint Julep

Collins Glass — Shaved Ice
11 oz.
2½ oz. Whiskey
12 Mint Leaves Muddled
1 tsp. Sugar
2½ oz. Water
Stir until ice melts
Add more ice to fill glass
Garnish with mint

NOTE:
Would be more popular but for the unavailability of the mint leaves.

Moscow Mule

Copper Mug ½ filled with Ice
8 oz.
1½ oz. Vodka
Pour Ginger Beer to fill up glass
Squeeze ½ Lime, drop juice and
lime into drink
Stir

NOTE:
Very popular in the '40s; respon-
sible for vodka's popularity.

Old Fashioned

Old Fashioned Glass filled with
Ice   7 oz.
½ oz. Simple Syrup
Dash Bitters
1 oz. Whiskey
Dash of Soda
Garnish with Cherry

NOTE:
You may prefer to muddle-mash
cherry in glass before anything
else is added.

Orange Blossom

Cocktail Glass rimmed with
Sugar   4½ oz.
Mixing Cup — Ice
1½ oz. Orange Juice
½ oz. Simple Syrup
1 oz. Gin
Blend and pour

NOTE:
Another delightful cocktail served
in a sugar-rimmed glass. An
appropriate dessert drink.

Orange Cadillac

Champagne Glass   4½ oz.
Mixing Cup, 4 oz. Ice
¼ oz. Galliano Liqueur
½ oz. White Creme de Cacao
1 oz. Cream
2 oz. Orange Juice
Blend and strain

NOTE:
Another delicious, fattening,
licorice- flavored cocktail.

Perfect Manhattan

Stemmed Manhattan or Rock
Glass   4 oz.
Fill glass ¾ with Ice
Dash of Sweet Vermouth
Dash of Dry Vermouth
1½ oz. Whiskey
Garnish with Lemon Twist and
drop peel into drink.

NOTE:

*Perfect Scotch same as Perfect
Manhattan except for the liquor.
The Perfect Manhattan is much
more popular than the Perfect
Martini.*

Perfect Martini

Cocktail Glass   4 oz.

Mixing Cup — 5 oz. Ice

1½ oz. Gin

½ oz. Dry Vermouth

½ oz. Sweet Vermouth

Stir and strain

Garnish with Olive or Lemon Twist.

NOTE:

A spin-off of the Martini. It should be more popular; a wonderfully different Martini.

Pina Colada

Collins Glass ½ filled with Ice
11 oz.
2 oz. Cream of Coconut Syrup
3 oz. Pineapple Juice
1 oz. Light Rum
Blend and Pour
Garnish with strip of Pineapple,
if desired.

NOTE:
Very popular in the Western
U.S.A. with people who like the
flavor of coconut.

Pineapple Champagne Cocktail

Champagne Glass   3½ oz.
½ oz. Heavy Pineapple Syrup
½ oz. Calvados
   (French Apple Brandy)
1 Cocktail Spear of Pineapple
Stir gently
Fill with Dry Champagne.

NOTE:
If Calvados is unavailable, Apple Jack or Apple Brandy may be substituted.

Pink Gin

Stemmed Manhattan or Rock
Glass   5 oz.
Fill glass ¾ with Ice
2 oz. Gin
2 Dashes Angostura Bitters
(Orange)

NOTE:
A teaspoon of cherry juice or
grenadine may be added to
enhance the color.

Pink Lady

Cocktail Glass   5½ oz.
Mixing Cup, 4 oz. Ice
2 oz. Cream
1 oz. Gin
½ oz. Grenadine
Blend and strain

NOTE:
Very popular with young people and ladies.

Pink Squirrel

Cocktail Glass rimmed with
Sugar   5½ oz.
1 oz. Creme de Noyaux or
        Creme de Almond
1 oz. White Creme de Cacao
¾ oz. Cream
Blend with ice and strain

NOTE:
Pinker and smoother than the
Pink Lady. Very popular with
ladies.

Planters Punch

Collins Glass ½ filled with Ice
11 oz.
Mixing Cup, Ice
1½ oz. Sweet Lemon Juice
Dash of Bitters
½ oz. Grenadine
1 oz. Dark Rum
Blend and pour
Fill with Soda
Garnish with Cherry

NOTE:
Very popular with old-time drinkers. Recipe started on Myers's Rum bottle.

Pousse Café

Cordial Glass   1½ oz.

¼ oz. Cherry Herring

¼ oz. Green Creme de Menthe

¼ oz. White Creme de Menthe

¼ oz. Brown Creme de Cacao

¼ oz. Creme de Banana

¼ oz. Tuaca

Top with Cream if desired

Pour liqueur carefully over back of spoon; clean spoon between layers.

NOTE:
This drink will layer for a pretty effect. The heaviest liqueurs first, etc. An exercise in frustration for an amateur bartender. The trick to keeping the layers separated is knowing the weights of the liqueurs.

Puerto Rican Pink Lady

Cocktail Glass   5½ oz.

Mixing Cup, 4 oz. Ice

1½ oz. Golden Rum

¾ oz. Lemon Juice

½ Egg White

¼ oz. Grenadine

Blend slow speed 15 seconds.

Pour into sugar-rimmed glass.

NOTE:

The egg white and rum is the difference between Puerto Rican Pink Lady and the regular Pink Lady.

Ramos Fizz

Collins Glass   11 oz.

Mixing Cup, 4 oz. Ice

2 oz. Sweet Lemon Juice

½ oz. Cream

1 oz. Gin

2 Dashes Orange Flower Water

1 Egg White

Fill with Soda

Blend and Pour

Garnish with Orange Slice if served in the afternoon or evening.

NOTE:
A great pick-me-up the morning after the night before.

Rob Roy (Scotch Manhattan)

Rock Glass filled with Ice   5 oz.
1 oz. Scotch
¼ oz. Sweet Vermouth
Dash of Bitters
Garnish with Cherry or Olive

NOTE:
A scotch drinkers' favorite
throughout the U.S.A.

Rum and Coconut Cooler

Collins Glass   14 oz.
Mixing Cup, 4 oz. Ice
2½ oz. Light Rum
1 oz. Creme de Coconut
½ oz. Lemon Juice
Blend and strain
Garnish with Lemon slice and
Cherry.

NOTE:
This must be tried by Easterners.
Very popular in the Southwest.

Rum and Coke

Highball Glass filled with Ice
8 oz.
1 oz. Light Rum
Fill with Coke

NOTE:
Tasty, simple, universally called
for. Dark Rum may be used in
this drink to save the Light Rum
for drinks you don't want
discolored.

Rusty Nail

Old Fashioned Glass, Ice   5½ oz.
¾ oz. Scotch
¾ oz. Drambuie
Pour over rocks in glass
Stir and serve

NOTE:
*For the sophisticated drinker all
over the country.*

Salty Dog

Highball Glass filled with Ice
8 oz.
Salt rim of glass
1 oz. Vodka
Fill with Grapefruit Juice

NOTE:
A Greyhound with salt.

Sazerac

Old Fashioned Glass   5½ oz.
¼ tsp. Absinthe or substitute
½ tsp. Sugar
¼ tsp. Bitters
2 oz. Bourbon
1 tbsp. Water
Mix, add ice cube
Garnish with Lemon Peel Twist

NOTE:
Louisiana origination;
replacement of the regular Old
Fashioned down New Orleans
way.

Scorpion

Double Old Fashioned Glass
15 oz.
Mixing Cup, 4 oz. Ice
2 oz. Light Rum
2 oz. Orange Juice
½ oz. Lemon Juice
1 oz. Brandy
½ oz. Orgeat Syrup
Blend and strain
Add ice cubes to fill
Garnish with Orange Slice

NOTE:
Far superior to the Mai Tai,
in my opinion.

Scotch and Milk

Highball Glass filled with Ice
8 oz.
1 oz. Scotch
Fill to top with Milk

NOTE:
Very good hangover remedy for scotch drinkers.

Scotch Mist

Stemmed Manhattan or Rock
Glass   5½ oz.
½ filled with Crushed Ice
1 oz. Scotch Whisky
¼ oz. Irish Mist Liqueur

NOTE:
These two liqueurs marry quite
readily. Irish Mist Liqueur is
excellent by itself.

Screwdriver

Highball Glass ¾ filled with Ice
8 oz.
1 oz. Vodka
Fill with Orange Juice

Foamy Drink: Add ½ oz. cream
and blend.

NOTE:
*This drink, along with the
Moscow Mule, were responsible
for vodka's gaining popularity in
the U.S.A.*

Shirley Temple

Collins Glass ½ filled with Ice
11 oz.
4 oz. Sweet Lemon Juice
1 oz. Grenadine
Fill up with Soda or 7-Up
Garnish with Cherry and
Orange Slice

NOTE:
For non-alcohol drinkers and
children. Many variations.

Side Car

Cocktail Glass rimmed with
Powdered Sugar
Mixing Cup, 4 oz. Ice
1½ oz. Sweet Lemon Juice
½ oz. Triple Sec
1 oz. Brandy
Blend and strain

NOTE:
This cocktail is said to be in the
first 20 cocktails ever made in
the U.S.A. Considered very fancy;
few modern-day bartenders are
familiar with it.

Silver Fizz

Collins Glass ½ filled with Ice
11 oz.
Mixing Cup, Ice
2 oz. Sweet Lemon Juice
1 Egg White
1 oz. Gin
Blend and strain
Top with Soda

Golden Fizz: Use egg yolk
Royal Fizz: Use white and yolk
of egg

NOTE:
An easy way to separate egg
white: break a ½-inch hole in
small end of the egg tip and pour
out the egg white.

Singapore Sling

Collins Glass ½ filled with Ice

11 oz.

Mixing Cup, Ice

1½ oz. Sweet Lemon Juice

½ oz. Grenadine

1 oz. Gin

Blend and pour

Fill with Soda

Pour ½ oz. Cherry Brandy on top

Garnish with Cherry

NOTE:

An old and beautiful cocktail. A drink that probably holds the record for being made incorrectly. The above recipe is the correct one.

Sloe Gin Fizz

Collins Glass ¾ filled with Ice
11 oz.
2 oz. Sweet Lemon Juice
1 oz. Sloe Gin
Blend and pour
Fill with Soda
Garnish with Cherry

NOTE:
Because of their festive nature,
fizzes are delightful to serve at
home.

Sloe Screw

Highball Glass, Ice   8 oz.
1½ oz. Sloe Gin
Fill to top with Orange Juice
Stir

Can blend if foam is desired.

NOTE:
This drink is popular in the urban areas.

Smoky Martini

Cocktail Glass   3½ oz.
Mixing Cup, 5 oz. Ice
1½ oz. Gin
¼ oz. Dry Vermouth
¼ oz. Scotch
Stir and strain
Garnish with olive

NOTE:
The touch of Scotch is the smoke.

Sombrero

Highball Glass filled with Ice
8 oz.
1 oz. Coffee-flavored Brandy or
Liqueur
Fill with Milk, stir, and serve

NOTE:
Popular in parts of Southwest
U.S.A.

Southern Comfort Manhattan

Stemmed Manhattan or Rock
Glass
¾ filled with Ice   5½ oz.
1½ oz. Southern Comfort
¼ oz. Dry Vermouth
Stir and garnish with Cherry

NOTE:
This is a mellow drink. The dry
vermouth neutralizes the extreme
sweetness of the Southern
Comfort.

Stinger

Stemmed Manhattan or Rock
Glass
½ filled with Ice   5½ oz.
1½ oz. Brandy
½ oz. White Creme de Menthe

NOTE:
Pour brandy into glass first.
The Creme de Menthe will sink
through brandy to the bottom.
Green Creme de Menthe can be
used if requested.

Tahiti Club

Old Fashioned Glass   5½ oz.
Mixing Cup, 4 oz. Ice
2 oz. Golden Rum
½ oz. Lime Juice
¾ oz. Pineapple Juice
½ oz. Lemon Juice
⅛ oz. Grenadine
Blend and strain
Garnish with Orange slice

NOTE:
You can multiply recipe and blend 5 at a time: 10 seconds on blender will suffice.

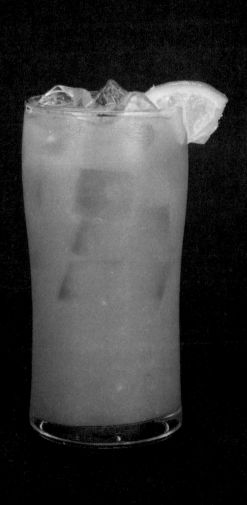

Tequila Sunrise

Collins Glass ½ filled with Ice
11 oz.
½ oz. Curacao (Orange)
1 oz. Tequila
2½ oz. Orange Juice
Fill almost to top with Soda
Top with ½ oz. Grenadine
Garnish with Lime slice

NOTE:
Became very popular in the west
first and spread all over the
U.S.A.

Tom and Jerry

Mug or Tumbler   8 oz.
2 oz. Brandy
½ oz. Rum
1 Egg — yolk and white beaten
      separately
1 tsp. Granulated Sugar
Mix yolk and white of egg into
mug
Add Sugar
Add Rum and Brandy
Fill with Hot Milk or Water
Nutmeg on top

NOTE:
Fine drink to serve on cool days;
quite tasty.
Except for the addition of the hot
milk or hot water, this drink
could be made in advance of your
party.

Tom Collins

Collins Glass ½ filled with Ice
11 oz.
2½ oz. Sweet Lemon Juice
1 oz. Gin
Fill with Soda
Garnish with Cherry

NOTE:
*Another cocktail very easily
made. Nationally popular.*

Velvet Hammer

Cocktail Glass   5½ oz.
Mixing Cup, Ice
¾ oz. White Creme de Cacao
¾ oz. Triple Sec
¾ oz. Cream
Blend and strain

NOTE:
Excellent cocktail for very light drinkers. Very low alcohol content.

Vesuvius

Cordial Glass   1 oz.
¾ oz. Brown Creme de Cacao
¼ oz. Green Chartreuse
Place Chartreuse on top by
pouring over spoon.
Flame in glass. To ignite drink,
hold flame under ½ teaspoon of
Chartreuse, ignite glass with
flaming spoon.
Allow glass to cool before
tasting.

NOTE:
Replace Creme de Cacao with
Vodka and you have a Green
Lizard.

Vodka Collins

Tall Collins Glass   11 oz.
Mixing Cup, 5 oz. Ice
2 oz. Sweet Lemon Juice
1 oz. Vodka
Blend and pour
Fill Glass with Soda

NOTE:
Same as Tom Collins except for liquor and the Tom Collins isn't blended.
The Vodka Collins may be requested sweeter or dryer.

Vodka Gimlet

Stemmed Manhattan or Rock
Glass,
Ice   5½ oz.
1½ oz. Vodka
½ oz. Rose's Lime Juice
Garnish with piece of Lime

This is on the rocks; you may
choose to stir to chill and strain.

NOTE:
*If mixing cup is used, stir slightly
longer than the martini to chill
better. The Rose's Lime Juice can
stand the added water from the
melted ice without taking
anything away from the cocktail.*

Ward 8

Highball Glass   8 oz.
Mixing Cup, 4 oz. Ice
2 oz. Whiskey
½ oz. Lemon Juice
1 tsp. Sugar
½ tsp. Grenadine
Blend and strain
Garnish with Lemon slice

NOTE:
A universal favorite; very attractive, tasty cocktail.

Watermelon Cooler

Collins Glass   14 oz.

Mixing Cup, 3 oz. Ice

½ cup Watermelon

2 oz. Light Rum

½ oz. Rose's Lime Juice

¼ oz. Maraschino Liqueur

1 tsp. Sugar

Pour and add ice cubes to fill

Garnish with slice of Lime

NOTE:

Popular in the southeastern part of the U.S.A. Originated in Georgia.

Whiskey Sour

Sour Glass   4½ oz.
Mixing Cup, 3 oz. Ice
2 oz. Sweet Lemon Juice
1 oz. Whiskey
Blend and strain
Garnish with Cherry and Orange
slice speared on same pick

NOTE:
All Sours are the same except for
liquor used.
This is a very popular drink all
over the U.S.A. with both women
and men.

White Russian

Manhattan or Rock Glass ¾
filled with Ice   5½ oz.
1½ oz. Vodka
½ oz. Kahlua
Top with Cream
Place swizzle stick in drink

NOTE:
Same recipe as the Black
Russian except for the cream.

Supplement of Recipes

Kama Kazi

Cordial Glass
Mixing cup ½ Filled with
  Fine Ice
¾ oz. Vodka

¼ oz. Lime Juice
Stir & Strain

Salty Dog
(original)

Highball Glass—
  (Moisten Rim So Your
  Salt Will Stick to Glass)
Fill with Ice

1 oz. Gin
Fill with Grapefruit Juice
Stir and Serve

Separator

Highball Glass—
  Filled with Ice
1 oz. Brandy
1 oz. Kahlua or Tia Maria

Fill with Cream or
  ½ & ½ Milk
Stir and Serve

Climax

Cocktail or Champagne
  Glass
Mixing Cup ¼ Filled
  with Ice
½ oz. Amaretto
½ oz. White Creme
  de Cacao
½ oz. Triple Sec

½ oz. Vodka
½ oz. Creme de Banana
1 oz. Cream
Blend and Strain.

Fogcutter

Collins Glass Filled
  with Ice
Mixing Cup 3 oz. Ice
½ oz. Brandy
½ oz. Gin

½ oz. Light Rum
1 oz. Sweet & Sour
3 oz. Pineapple Juice
Blend, Strain and Serve—
  Lime or Lemon Garnish.

French
Connection

Rock or Old Fashion Glass
  Filled with Ice
1 oz. Brandy

½ oz. Amaretto or
  Tia Maria
Stir and Serve.

Liqueurs

Abisante, Light green Anise or Licorice flavored

Abricots, Creme of Apricot

Absinthe, Made from wormwood. Illegal now
because of its reputation as an aphrodisiac.

Advocaat, Egg Liqueur from Holland

Amer Picon, French bitter aperitif

Chartreuse, Green or Light Yellow—110 proof

Cassis, made from black currants

Cherry Suisse, chocolate and cherry flavored

Cointreau, similar to Triple Sec

Curacao, made from small green orange peel
and spices

Czasakorte, Hungarian pear

Gebirgs Enzian, made from gentian root

Glayua, Scotland, honey, herbs, anise, licorice
flavored

Grand Marnier, France, orange and Cognac

Gold Wasser, orange flavored with 22 carat gold in
liqueur (health drink)

Herb Saint, substitute for Absinthe, no poisonous
wormwood

Irish Mist, Irish whiskey and honey

Kirsch Liqueur, sweet white cherry flavor

Kummel, sweet caraway flavor

Likier Smaku Ozynowego, Blackberry flavored not
heavy with sugar

Maraschino, A white liqueur of black cherries
and pits

Noyaux, made from many different fruit pits, almond flavor

Ouzo, Greek National Liqueur 90 proof licorice flavored

Reishu, melon flavored

Roiano, Anise and vanilla

Sabra, Jewish. Orange and chocolate

Sloe Gin, red made from sloe plums of the black thorn-bush

Southern Comfort, whiskey and peach usually 100 proof

Tea Breeze, tea flavored

Triple Sec, colorless orange flavored sometimes with orange flower water

Tuaca, milk brandy orange flavor, slight coconut

Zitronen Eis, lemon liqueur

BARTENDER'S REFERENCES

BARTENDER'S REFERENCES